Facilitator's Guide

Failure Is NOT an Option®

Second Edition

Facilitator's Guide

Failure Is NOT an Option®

6 Principles for Making Student Success the *ONLY* Option

Second Edition

ALAN M. BLANKSTEIN

A JOINT PUBLICATION

CORWIN
A SAGE Company

HOPE
Foundation

For information:

Corwin
A SAGE Company
2455 Teller Road
Thousand Oaks, California 91320
(800) 233-9936
Fax: (800) 417-2466
www.corwinpress.com

SAGE India Pvt. Ltd.
B 1/I 1 Mohan Cooperative
    Industrial Area
Mathura Road, New Delhi 110 044
India

SAGE Ltd.
1 Oliver's Yard
55 City Road
London EC1Y 1SP
United Kingdom

SAGE Asia-Pacific Pte. Ltd.
33 Pekin Street #02-01
Far East Square
Singapore 048763

Printed in the United States of America

ISBN: 978-1-4129-8174-3

This book is printed on acid-free paper.

09   10   11   12   13   10 9 8 7 6 5 4 3 2 1

Acquisitions Editor:	Debra Stollenwerk
Associate Editor:	Julie McNall
Editorial Assistant:	Allison Scott
Developmental Editor:	Daniel J. Richcreek
Production Editor:	Melanie Birdsall
Copy Editor:	Adam Dunham
Typesetter:	C&M Digitals (P) Ltd.
Proofreader:	Cheryl Rivard
Cover Designer:	Karine Hovsepian

Contents

Resources

About the Author

Alan M. Blankstein is Founder and President of the HOPE (Harnessing Optimism and Potential through Education) Foundation, a not-for-profit organization, the Honorary Chair of which is Nobel Prize winner Archbishop Desmond Tutu. The HOPE Foundation is dedicated to supporting educational leaders over time in creating school cultures where failure is not an option for *any* student. Founded in 1989, the HOPE Foundation has focused for the past decade on helping districts build leadership capacity to close gaps and sustain student success.

The HOPE Foundation launched the professional learning communities movement in educational circles first by bringing W. Edwards Deming and later Peter Senge to light in a series of Shaping America's Future forums and PBS video conferences from 1989 to 1992. The HOPE Foundation now provides some 20 conferences annually, highlighting their long-term successes in sustaining student achievement in districts and regions in 17 states and parts of Canada and South Africa.

A former "high risk" youth, Alan began his career in education as a music teacher and has worked in youth-serving organizations since 1983, including the March of Dimes, Phi Delta Kappa, and the National Educational Service (now Solution Tree), which he founded in 1987 and directed for 12 years.

In addition to authorship of this award-winning book, Alan is publisher of three *Failure Is Not an Option* video series and, with Paul Houston, is senior editor of the 13-volume *The Soul of Educational Leadership* series. Alan also coauthored the *Reaching Today's Youth* curriculum and has published articles in *Educational Leadership, The School Administrator, Executive Educator, High School Magazine, Reaching Today's Youth*, and *Inside the Workshop*. Alan has also provided keynote presentations and workshops for virtually every major educational organization.

Alan served on the Harvard International Principals Centers advisory board, as board member for Federation of Families for

Children's Mental Health, as Co-Chair of Indiana University's Neal Marshall Black Culture Center's Community Network, and as advisor to the Faculty and Staff for Student Excellence (FASE) mentoring program. He also served as advisory board member for the Forum on Race, Equity, and Human Understanding with the Monroe County Schools in Indiana and on the Board of Trustees for the Jewish Child Care Agency (JCAA), in which he was once a youth in residence.

How to Use This Chapter-by-Chapter Guide

Failure Is Not an Option *addresses all the elements that are absolutely necessary for effective and enduring educational reform. It is a deeply passionate call to arms, combined with the wherewithal to take systematic, continuous, and effective action. A must-read for all those interested in reform because it is simultaneously inspiring and practical.*

—Michael Fullan, University of Toronto

This Facilitator's Guide is a companion to *Failure Is Not an Option: 6 Principles for Making Student Success the ONLY Option,* Second Edition, a book that tells the vivid story of what it takes to turn schools around, continually improve schools that are already good, and succeed with ALL students. Drawing on more than 15 years of practical research, and an in-depth look at 20 high-performing schools and districts, the book identifies six principles that guide sustainable professional learning communities. Most important, readers will find a detailed set of field-tested processes for re-creating these successes in their own schools.

Many schools are choosing this accessible publication for collaborative book study groups. Most groups will read one or two chapters before each group meeting. This simple guide is structured to help the leader facilitate those meetings.

For each meeting, a set of *chapter content review* questions will help readers prepare for the group meeting by highlighting the main points of each chapter. Readers may want to write down answers to the questions beforehand and take them to the group meeting.

Suggested group *activities* are designed for small or large groups but can be undertaken by individuals working alone. In advance of each meeting, decide which activities you will be pursuing together and which activities members will be encouraged to do on their own.

The open-ended *discussion* questions are designed to encourage members both to apply what they have read to their own experiences or current professional concerns and to share these with their colleagues. In some cases, you may want to look at the discussion questions first and then undertake the activities, or you may want to alternate between activities and discussion. In every case, the activities and discussion questions are meant to be suggestions only. Each group leader may decide to skip some, add others, or amend all to fit local issues.

There are suggestions *for further reading* for practitioners who wish to pursue a topic in greater depth individually or for group members to assign in round-robin fashion so that each member reads and summarizes a selection during the series of meetings.

Finally, at the back of this guide are all of the *resources* that accompany this guide and the main text. Each of these resources is included in the activities and discussion question of their corresponding chapters. As facilitator, you may want to have copies of these available in each meeting, as they are not found in the main text. However, they are also available to all participants through the HOPE Foundation Web site at www.hopefoundation.org.

Note: Chapter 5 is longer and more complex than the others. You may want to schedule extra time for the meeting at which it is discussed, or discuss it over two successive meetings.

Tips to Facilitate Discussion

☐ Read the material in advance, and budget time for each portion of the study.

☐ Use a model of team facilitation. Two facilitators can keep the conversation interesting, and each often engages the study group in different ways. In addition, expand the opportunity for leadership to include everyone who is willing to lead.

☐ Use a full range of visual aids. Instead of having participants write on paper only, use an overhead projector, computer, flip chart, marker board, or other tools. Ask participants to help.

☐ If your study is not done in a single session but extends over a period of time, get contact information for all participants and communicate with them between study dates. This can be useful to remind participants of the next study and to refresh their memory of the previous topics discussed.

☐ For ongoing study, create a space on the Internet or intranet where participants can add comments and collaborate.

☐ Send participants meeting details in advance, including *study questions* and a schedule of *what to read* for each meeting. Also, send a reminder of what is expected of participants a couple days before each meeting.

☐ Select a location that is comfortable, such as a participant's home or casual meeting room. A location other than school can be more inviting and contribute to a better meeting experience. Be sure, however, that enough space is available to break into smaller groups if necessary.

☐ Include light refreshments as an extra feature for a meeting. Serve the refreshments at different times during the meeting. Participants can contribute.

☐ Make the study relevant to the group's experiences. You do not have to limit the discussion to the questions in the study guide.

❏ Take a break during the meeting for personal conversations.

❏ Do an opening icebreaker. It helps start a more relaxing meeting. Keep the icebreaker informal: Ask everyone to introduce themselves and tell a brief funny story from their teaching experience.

❏ Take time to reflect and summarize at the conclusion of the meeting.

❏ Respect everyone's time. If some participants were too busy to read the book in advance, do not waste time in the seminar allowing them to catch up. The Chapter Content Review should fill them in on the main topics.

❏ Collect filled-in Workshop Evaluation Forms from the participants at the conclusion of the meeting and use their comments for ongoing improvement of future meetings.

❏ Some of the later chapters are longer and/or more involved. Depending on the time available, you may want to break into smaller groups, each ideally made up of staff from the same school or level (e.g., elementary or middle schools). Each group could then participate in activities only most applicable to them.

Additional Resources for Facilitators

Corwin also offers a free 16-page resource titled *Tips for Facilitators*, which includes practical strategies and tips for guiding a successful meeting. The information in this section describes different professional development opportunities, the principles of effective professional development, some characteristics of an effective facilitator, the responsibilities of the facilitator, and practical tips and strategies to make the meeting more successful. *Tips for Facilitators* is available for free download at the Corwin Web site (www.corwin press.com, under "Resources/Tips for Facilitators").

We recommend that facilitators download a copy of *Tips for Facilitators* and review the characteristics and responsibilities of facilitators and professional development strategies for different types of work groups and settings.

Chapter-by-Chapter Study Guide

Failure Is Not an Option:
6 Principles for Making Student
Success the ONLY Option, **Second Edition**

By Alan M. Blankstein

Chapter 1. Why Failure Is Not an Option

Chapter Content Review

1. Name two primary reasons why failure is not an option in education.
2. Discuss the single most important element for success in any endeavor as listed on page 5.

Activities

1. In no more than two sentences, complete the following statement: "I decided to become an educator because . . ." Share and discuss your response with others in your study group. You may want to form smaller groups of two or three for this activity.
2. List on a board or overhead the six lessons learned beginning on page 12. In small groups, have participants discuss the lesson that most inspired them as they read this chapter. This is a good way for participants to get to know one another. Have each group discuss their particular situations—and how you would like to see them change.
3. As a group, complete Resource 1, FNO Snapshot Rubric for Educational Leaders, and Resource 2, FNO Student-Success Model and Critical-Success Factors, to get an overview of the school's current status (if multiple schools are represented in the group, divide the group by school affiliation for this exercise). You will refer to these forms in Chapter 10.
4. Review Case Story 1, Six Lessons Exemplified Across a Region. In small groups, brainstorm some of the things your school or district can do to increase relationships within your school and across your district and other districts. How could these plans be implemented? What would you like to learn from other districts? What do you feel your school or district has to offer?

Discussion

1. On page 3, there is a quote from Michael Fullan, "A high-quality public school system is essential." As a group, brainstorm ways in which educators can help make each of these 10 things possible (you can use this in future discussions as the group reads more of the book).
2. The author poses the question, "*Why* are we in this profession?" (page 5). Why, according to him, is this question key to any successful improvement effort?
3. Hand out copies of Resources 3 through 6, found at the back of this Facilitator's Guide. As a group, review and discuss each. How can you use each of these? Which would be most useful in your school or district?

4. Consider the "Think It Through..." questions on page 28 about "Six Lessons Learned at Williamston Middle Schools." Answer each of these questions as a group.

Further Reading

Fullan, M. G. (2003). *Change forces with a vengeance.* New York: Routledge/Falmer.

Heifetz, R. (1999). *Leadership without easy answers.* Cambridge, MA: Belknap Press of Harvard University Press.

Stoll, L., & Temperley, J. (2009). Creative leadership: A challenge of our times. *School Leadership and Management, 29*(1), 63–76.

Resources

Resource 1. FNO Snapshot Rubric for Educational Leaders
Resource 2. FNO Student-Success Model and Critical-Success Factors
Resource 3. Williamston Zoomerang Survey: Tying Professional Development to Results
Resource 4. FNO Tuning Protocol
Resource 5. Williamston Graphic Organizer and Rubric for Writing
Resource 6. Williamston Professional Development Agenda

Chapter 2. Courageous Leadership for School Success

Chapter Content Review

1. The author defines the *courageous leadership imperative* as "acting in accordance with one's own values, beliefs, and mission" (page 31). Explain what the author means by this definition.
2. List the five axioms characterizing courageous leadership and examples of each.

Activities

1. Break into five smaller groups, assigning each group one of the five axioms. Ask each group to list five ways these axioms apply to their experiences. Then have each group present their findings to the group as a whole.
2. List the three cited principles of highly reliable organizations (HROs) shown on page 34. Break up into smaller groups and have each group give examples of specifics that schools could change to better meet these principles.
3. Three activities are suggested on pages 39 to 40 that can help leaders reflect on their core values and ideals. As a group, decide in advance which you will undertake and whether you will attempt the activities alone before your next meeting (e.g., the three questions listed on page 39) or together as a group (the activities involving pairs and triads suggested on page 39).

Discussion

1. How do you respond to the idea that the education of the young is a moral issue?
2. Respond to the following statement: "Leaders who overturn long-held assumptions and traditions to direct their schools and students toward a better future often face strong resistance in the school, district, and larger community."
3. From your own experience, what are some reasons why leading change requires courage?
4. What might help skeptical, cynical, or burned-out educators recoup the idealism that led most of them into the profession at the beginning of their careers?

Further Reading

Covey, S. R. (1989). *The 7 habits of highly effective people.* New York: Simon & Schuster.

Darling-Hammond, L. (1997). *The right to learn: A blueprint for creating schools that work.* San Francisco: Jossey-Bass.

Evans, R. (1996). *The human side of school change.* San Francisco: Jossey-Bass.

Fullan, M. G. (2003). *The moral imperative of school leadership.* Thousand Oaks, CA: Corwin.

Glickman, C. (2003). *Holding sacred ground: Essays on leadership, courage, and endurance in our schools.* San Francisco: Jossey-Bass.

Livsey, R. C., & Palmer, P. J. (1999). *The courage to teach: A guide for reflection and renewal.* San Francisco: Jossey-Bass.

Chapter 3. 10 Common Routes to Failure, and How to Avoid Each

Chapter Content Review

1. List on a board or overhead the 10 common routes to failure and examples of how to avoid each.
2. Cite examples of ways the Alton School District and Nancy Duden at Kate Sullivan Elementary School overcame these obstacles to progress.

Activities

1. Review Resource 7, Strategies for Making Time, on page 40 of this guide. Then, in groups of three or four, brainstorm additional strategies and discuss ways that some of these strategies could be implemented in your schools.
2. Complete Resource 8, Self-Assessment, on pages 41 through 44 of this guide. (District administrators might answer in terms of the district as a whole.) Discuss your ratings with other members of the group. Is there a consensus in your group about some of the negative ratings? What does this assessment tell you?
3. Recall any improvement efforts you have been involved with or have witnessed. Share these experiences with other group members. How did the 10 obstacles affect the improvement efforts under discussion?
4. In small groups, discuss other ways the 10 obstacles can be avoided. How has each group or members of each group avoided these obstacles in the past? Were their methods effective? What could they have done differently to better avoid these obstacles?

Discussion

1. As a group, discuss the questions on page 56 about Case Story 2, Alton Community School District Chooses a New Direction. Did most participants (including the facilitator) see the same obstacles as being the closest to their situation? How did their perspectives differ?
2. Review Resource 9, Strategies for Dealing With Resistance, on page 45 of this guide. Share and discuss incidents when the listed "ineffective behaviors" (page 45 of this guide) demolished well-designed improvement initiatives.

3. Recall and share situations in which you encountered resistance to a change or improvement you espoused, or describe a planned change that is likely to arouse resistance. How could the use of any of the strategies listed on page 45 of this guide affect your chances of implementing the change?

Further Reading

Blankstein, A. M., & Swain, H. (1994, February). Is TQM right for schools? *The Executive Educator, 16*(2), 51–54.

Darling-Hammond, L. (1996). The quiet revolution: Rethinking teacher development. *Educational Leadership, 53*(6), 4–10.

Fullan, M. G. (2001). *Leading in a culture of change.* San Francisco: Jossey-Bass.

Fullan, M. G. (2004). *Leading in a culture of change: Personal action guide and workbook.* New York: John Wiley.

Southworth, G. (2009). *Courageous leadership for shaping America's future: A synthesis of best practices guiding school leadership for 21st century education.* Bloomington, IN: HOPE Foundation.

Resources

Resource 7. Strategies for Making Time
Resource 8. Self-Assessment
Resource 9. Strategies for Dealing With Resistance

Chapter 4. Relational Trust as Foundation for the Learning Community

Chapter Content Review

1. Define *relational trust* and list its four components.
2. Articulate the concept or definition of *learning community* that characterizes an ideal school community.

Activities

1. In small groups, review the four questions found on page 73. Have each group present their answers to the group as a whole. Afterward, try to combine everyone's answers into a comprehensive list that can be posted at the front of the room. Return to it after you've completed the chapter. How would the group change this list?
2. In small groups, look over the items in the box Trust and the Learning Community on page 73. Analyze each to show how the described situation reflects, or is founded on, a trusting interpersonal relationship. (You may skip the item about SMART goals, which will be taken up in the next chapter.) Consider whether the same situations would be found in your own school.

Discussion

1. Consider, in turn, each of the six principles that the author proposes as the essence of a professional learning community (page 81). What, if anything, do you believe may have been left out? List any suggested omissions. After you have finished the book, decide whether those items you thought were missing were subsumed under one of the principles discussed in the remaining chapters.
2. Discuss instances in which talented administrators (superintendents or principals) failed to gain the trust of those working under them. What were some of the elements in the personal relationships that led to this failure?

Further Reading

Barth, R. S. (2001). *Learning by heart*. San Francisco: Jossey-Bass.

Bryk, A. S., & Schneider, B. (2002). *Trust in schools: A core resource for improvement*. New York: Russell Sage.

Hargreaves, A. (2003). *Teaching in the knowledge society.* New York: Teachers College Press.

Murphy, J., Jost, J., & Shipman, N. (2000). Implementation of the interstate school leaders licensure consortium standards. *International Journal of Leadership in Education, 3*(1), 17–39.

Chapter 5. Principle 1: Common Mission, Vision, Values, and Goals

Chapter Content Review

1. Name the "four pillars of any organization"—the foundation blocks of its culture—and define each.
2. Describe what "good" looks like for each of the four pillars.
3. Describe ways to implement each of the four pillars.

Activities

Note: Due to the length of this chapter's activities, consider breaking into smaller groups with each group focusing on one or two of the following activities, or use two group meetings to address the activities and questions below.

1. Review the four questions listed on page 85 and the content of Figure 5.1 on page 92. With these questions and characteristics in mind, critique your own school's or district's mission statement. Then look at the bulleted items on page 94. How many of the listed strategies for keeping your mission statement alive are you currently using? List any other strategies you can think of.
2. Read and consider the "Think It Through . . ." questions on page 102. If your school or district has a vision statement, critique it using the criteria on page 96 and the general characteristics in Figure 5.2 on page 98. If your organization has no vision statement, write statements that you might include if you were asked to write one.
3. Discuss, define, and list the values implicit in your school's or district's culture. If you have existing mission and vision statements, refer to them. Examine each implicit value that you list by asking, "Is this value consistent with our mission? Will this value help us realize our vision?"
4. Review the characteristics of SMART goals (Figure 5.3 on page 107). Review goals that your school or district has adopted and decide whether they are SMART.

Discussion

1. Review the mission statements found in Resource 10, Running River Elementary School Mission Statement, and Resource 11, Development Process for Mission, Vision, Values, and Goals.

Would the group consider these to be effective mission statements? How do they differ from the mission statement for your school?

2. In small or large groups, discuss whether you need to rewrite or revitalize your mission, vision, values, or goals. Decide what steps need to be taken to begin the process.

3. Discuss the types of peer-to-peer observation and support you see practiced in your school or district. How often do you see this type of support in your school or district? Name several ways you and your colleagues could offer regular support to peers.

4. While reviewing the bulleted items on page 109, discuss the kinds of events and achievements that are typically celebrated in your school. Should you rethink your policies and start celebrating other kinds of successes? Where should you begin?

Further Reading

Barth, R. (2001). *Learning by heart*. San Francisco: Jossey-Bass.

DuFour, R., & Eaker, R. (1998). *Professional learning communities at work: Best practices for enhancing student achievement.* Bloomington, IN: National Educational Service.

Hord, S. M. (2003). *Learning together, leading together: Changing schools through professional learning communities.* New York: Teachers College Press, and Oxford, OH: National Staff Development Council.

Kotter, J. (1996). *Leading change.* Boston: Harvard Business School Press.

Nanus, B. (1992). *Visionary leadership.* San Francisco: Jossey-Bass.

Resources

Resource 10. Running River Elementary School Mission Statement

Resource 11. Development Process for Mission, Vision, Values, and Goals

Chapter 6. Principle 2: Ensuring Achievement for All Students—Systems for Prevention and Intervention

Chapter Content Review

1. Name three common reasons that school communities fail to take responsibility for ensuring that *all* children learn and suggest ways of addressing these.
2. List some traditional ways of diagnosing problem students and dealing with their misbehavior. Describe the four Cs of the Community Circle of Caring's alternative approach and how they promote connection versus disconnection.
3. Describe the five components of a comprehensive system for assuring the success of all students and review the examples given for each.

Activities

1. In small groups, preferably comprising staff at the same school or at the same grade-level range (e.g., all middle school), answer the questions in Resource 12, Worksheet for Developing a School Improvement Plan, on page 53 of this guide.
2. Form at least four small groups. Each group should sketch out a plan for answering the questions under one of the four topics in Resource 14, Developing a System of Prevention and Intervention, on pages 57 through 58 of this guide. Begin work on each topic by listing programs already in place and discussing their adequacy.
3. Break into small groups and discuss some of the mechanisms and prevention systems that are already in place for your students. How do these help to identify those who are at risk for academic difficulties? What else could your school or district do to help identify struggling students early on?
4. Break into small groups to discuss the "Think It Through . . ." questions on page 130. Once the groups have answered these questions, ask them to answer the following question: What systems could be put into place to help your incoming students? What steps would be involved in implementing these systems?

Discussion

1. Characterize the prevailing beliefs of your colleagues and staff about the power of teachers to ensure that all students are successful. How has staff behavior that reflects these beliefs affected student achievement, for better or for worse?

2. Review Case Story 5, RtI and Pyramid of Support at a Middle Class Suburban Elementary School, starting on page 135. How could your school or district use Resource 13, Pyramid of Support at Coyote Ridge Elementary School, on pages 54 to 56 of this guide to create and implement an effective plan of action?

3. Review the case example Confronting Behaviors on page 115. As a group, discuss the questions in the "Think It Through . . ." box on page 116, concentrating most of your time on the last question. Contrast this with the following question: How *should* leaders respond to behaviors that conflict with the school's or district's vision, mission, and values?

4. Review Figure 6.5 on page 126. Which column describes the practices in your school? What can you do to ensure that your policies fall in the left-hand column?

Further Reading

Blankstein, A. M., DuFour, R., & Little, M. (1997). *Reaching today's students.* Bloomington, IN: National Educational Service.

Brendtro, L. K., Brokenleg, M., & Bockern, S. V. (1990). *Reclaiming youth at risk: Our hope for the future.* Bloomington, IN: National Educational Services.

Darling-Hammond, L., & Bransford, J. (Eds.). (2005). *Preparing teachers for a changing world: What teachers should learn and be able to do.* San Francisco: Jossey-Bass.

Evans, R. (1996). *The human side of school change.* San Francisco: Jossey-Bass.

Noer, D. M. (1993). *Healing the wounds.* San Francisco: Jossey-Bass.

Resources

Resource 12. Worksheet for Developing a School Improvement Plan

Resource 13. Pyramid of Support at Coyote Ridge Elementary School

Resource 14. Developing a System of Prevention and Intervention

Chapter 7. Principle 3: Collaborative Teaming Focused on Teaching for Learning

Chapter Content Review

1. Describe characteristics of a culture of collaboration and list areas in which such teaming may occur.
2. List some of the protocols for teamwork that need to be decided for effective collaboration.
3. Review the eight implementation guidelines on pages 157 to 159 and the steps involved in each.

Activities

1. In small groups, discuss some challenges to creating a collaborative culture. What suggestions does the book give for ways these can be addressed? What other ways can these challenges be addressed? What ways has your school used in the past?
2. Consider the meetings of your study group for this book. Are there protocols you could establish to make your meetings more productive and useful? In small groups, draw up a set of rules for the rest of your meetings. Share these with the group and decide which of them you will observe from now on.
3. Consider a problem affecting your school or district that could be addressed by an effective team that is interdisciplinary (within a single school) or across two or more schools. Draw up a proposal for such a team that includes a list of its members, its goal or purpose, the logistics of its meeting and timeframe, and the responsibilities of its members.
4. As a group, review Resource 15, Instructional Learning Walks, on pages 59 to 62 of this guide. How could your group use this activity? If possible, create time in your schedule to complete this activity and then as a group discuss your findings.

Discussion

1. Review the two case examples Collaborative Teaming in Action and Cross-Departmental Teaming on pages 146 and 155 and then consider the "Think It Through . . ." questions on page 156. What could be done on the individual level to improve these strategies? On a group level?
2. How can collaboration among teachers lead to a sharing of the instructional strengths of each of them?

3. Discuss ways that teams of middle and high school representatives can improve student learning and preparedness for high school work.

Further Reading

Barth, R. S. (2001). *Learning by heart*. San Francisco: Jossey-Bass.

Fullan, M., & Hargreaves, A. (1996). *What's worth fighting for out there?* New York: Teachers College Press.

Roberts, S. M., & Pruitt, E. Z. (2003). *Schools as professional learning communities: Collaborative activities and strategies for professional development*. Thousand Oaks, CA: Corwin.

Resources

Resource 15. Instructional Learning Walks

Chapter 8. Principle 4: Data-Based Decision Making for Continuous Improvement

Chapter Content Review

1. Name the kinds of data that should be collected; several ways it can be used effectively; who should review, analyze, and use this data; and what benefits this data can offer educators.
2. Describe characteristics of data that are useful for planning school improvement and ways that the collected data can be used.
3. List several obstacles or challenges to collecting, analyzing, and using data effectively and ways these can be confronted or resolved.
4. Review the three types of assessment, when they should be used, how they differ, and the type of feedback each offers. Include Resources 16 through 18 in your discussion.

Activities

Note: Due to the length of this chapter's activities, consider breaking into smaller groups with each group focusing on one or two of the following activities, or use two group meetings to address the activities and questions below.

1. Divide into three or four small groups assigning each group 3 or 4 of the case examples in this chapter (except Overcoming Fear of Data). Using these case examples as a stepping off point, have each group brainstorm lists of the kinds of data that could be collected from your school or district.
2. While still divided up, have each group determine the best ways to obtain the information you want (survey, focus groups, interviews, test scores, and so forth) or the sources of data that are currently available. When done, compare and discuss the results as a large group.
3. In small groups, have participants review Table 8.1, Collecting and Examining Data in Your School, on pages 189 through 190. Have each group come up with answers to the first three questions. Then, as a large group, compare the graphic organizers each group came up with. As a group (or as individuals), decide which organizer would work best for your school.
4. Review the three exchanges on pages 179 to 180 under the "What Good Looks Like" heading and answer the questions posed by the author at the beginning of the section. How do the answers you came up with as a group match the answers discussed by the authors? Why do you agree? Disagree?

Discussion

1. What data would you need to collect in order to determine the causes of poor reading scores among third graders? Eighth graders? What would you do differently to determine the cause of poor math scores?

2. In your opinion, how well do results of state tests reflect the quality of student learning? If you feel there is a discrepancy, what are some kinds of data you can collect or generate to determine what skills and knowledge the students have actually acquired?

3. Review the "Think It Through . . ." questions on page 170 and answer them as a group. How can your school or districts come up with ways of collecting needed data? (Your group can use the kinds of data discussed in the previous question to jump-start the "how" question.)

4. Review the "Think It Through . . ." questions on page 172 and answer them as a group. How do the answers to these questions affect how the group answered the previous two questions? How does the "who" affect the "what" and "how"?

Further Reading

Black, P., Harrison, C., Lee, C., Marshall, B., & Wiliam, D. (2003). *Assessment for learning: Putting it into practice.* Maidenhead, UK: Open University Press.

Fullan, M., & St. Germain, C. (2006). *Learning places: A field guide for improving the context of schooling.* Thousand Oaks, CA: Corwin.

McTighe, J., & Wiggins, G. (2004). *Understanding by design: Professional development workbook.* Alexandria, VA: Association for Supervision and Curriculum Development.

Reeves, D. B. (2002a). *Making standards work* (3rd ed.). Denver, CO: Advanced Learning Press.

Stiggins, R. (2004). *Student-involved assessment for learning* (4th ed.). Upper Saddle River, NJ: Prentice Hall.

Resources

Resource 16. Checklist for Using Diagnostic (Preteaching) Assessments

Resource 17. Checklist for Using Formative Assessments

Resource 18. Checklist for Using Summative Assessments

Chapter 9. Principle 5: Gaining Active Engagement From Family and Community

Alan M. Blankstein and Pedro A. Noguera

Chapter Content Review

1. Name the three key principles of positive school-family relationships. Name at least three things schools can do to address these key principles.
2. Name the benefits to the school and community gained by good school-family relationships.
3. List the National PTA's six standards for family involvement
4. Name several challenges or obstacles to establishing good ties between school and community and possible solutions for each.

Activities

Note: Due to the length of this chapter's activities, consider breaking into smaller groups with each group focusing on one or two of the following activities, or use two group meetings to address the activities and questions below.

1. Consider the questions in the "Think It Through . . ." section on page 197. In small groups, come up with a plan that answers these questions that could be implemented at your school.
2. In small groups, read and discuss the scenarios in the section "What Good Looks Like" on pages 202 to 203. Rate each on the quality of the interaction and give reasons why each deserves such a rating. Come back as a large group and discuss your ratings.
3. In small groups, draw three columns on a piece of paper.

   Column 1: List typical issues involving family responsibilities for their children's schooling (tardiness, absenteeism, incomplete homework, failure to sign homework or other forms, etc.).
   Column 2: Next to each, note the school's current policy in regard to the issue.
   Column 3: Note possible reasons for the problem.

   Discuss whether the established policies address the source of the problem effectively and what a more empathetic approach might involve.

4. Break into small groups, preferably by school, and discuss the questions under the "Getting Started" section on pages 205 through 206. Now consider the strategies listed below these questions. Which strategies would work best for your school? As a group, discuss your findings. What common problems did the groups have? What are some of the solutions to these problems?

Discussion

1. Discuss the questions in the "Think It Through . . ." section on page 194. What could be done to improve relationships with parents of different racial, socioeconomic, and linguistic backgrounds? How could your school make them feel more welcome or comfortable?
2. Discuss and rate the quality of your school's or district's relationship with the community. What particular policies or practices could be adopted by schools that do not have positive ties?
3. Share and discuss experiences of group members or their colleagues in attempting to reach out to, or draw in, family and community members. In cases where these efforts were unsuccessful or frustrating, what might have been done differently?
4. How do you respond to the idea of making school representatives more visible at community gathering places and events? What are some ways they could be made more visible? What else could be done at these events to improve school-community relationships?

Further Reading

Elias, M. J., Bryan, K., Patrikakou, E. N., & Weissberg, R. P. (2003). *Challenges in creating effective home-school partnerships in adolescence: Promising paths for collaboration.* Chicago: Collaborative for Academic, Social, and Emotional Learning.

Harris, A., & Goodall, J. (2008). Do parents know they matter? Engaging all parents in learning. *Educational Research, 50*(3), 277–289.

Hill, N. E., & Tyson, D. F. (2009). Parental involvement in middle school: A meta-analytic assessment of the strategies that promote achievement. *Developmental Psychology, 45*(3), 740–763.

Chapter 10. Principle 6: Building Sustainable Leadership Capacity

Alan M. Blankstein with Andy Hargreaves and Dean Fink

Chapter Content Review

1. Explain why building leadership capacity in a school or district should be a priority concern.
2. Name and define six different leadership styles and the effects each style has on the people around them.
3. Describe the benefits of having teachers as leaders and several leadership roles teachers can assume inside and outside the school.
4. Define or describe *sustainability* of leadership in educational institutions, and the role of instructional leadership, "distributed" leadership, and leadership succession.

Activities

1. List instances in your school or district in which teachers played leadership roles (obtaining grants for instructional initiatives; organizing professional study groups, mentoring programs, or other professional development activities; evaluating or developing curricula or local assessments, and so on). Brainstorm ways these teachers can be encouraged and supported in their efforts so that others may be encouraged to exercise similar leadership.
2. Using the definitions in Figure 10.1 on pages 213 to 214, have administrators or others in leadership roles in the group silently evaluate their own leadership styles and consider approaches to raise the style to an even more positive level. If they feel comfortable, they could discuss their self-evaluations with colleagues.
3. Review the "10 Things That Are Sustainable About You" on pages 234 to 235. Break up into small groups and assign each group two or three of these. Have each group come up with ideas of what the school or district could do to implement these changes. As a group, discuss each of these. Have each group present their ideas to the whole group and brainstorm further ideas.
4. Review the answers the group gave to Resource 1, FNO Snapshot Rubric for Educational Leaders, and Resource 2, FNO Student-Success Model and Critical-Success Factors, from Chapter 1 (or, if you broke up into groups for multiple schools, divide up into the same groups for this exercise). Does everyone in the group still believe this is a good overview of the current status of your school? What can you do to fix any shortcomings?

What have you and your school done already to fix some of these problems?

Discussion

1. Share experiences of improvement initiatives that floundered when leaders left. In retrospect, suggest steps the original leaders might have taken to ensure that the impetus for change was sustained.
2. If your group consists largely of administrators, share and discuss your reactions to the idea of sharing leadership and responsibility with teaching staff.
3. If the group is composed of teachers, discuss the kinds of instructional development or professional development leadership opportunities you would like to initiate and the kinds of support (time or other resources) you would require to do so.
4. Discuss the five implications listed by the author in the "Discussion and Conclusion" section starting on page 236. How well does this list fit into the goals of your school or district? How can your school's or district's goals be adjusted to include the ideas from this list?

Further Reading

Collins, J. (2001). *Good to great.* New York: HarperCollins.

Goleman, D., Boyatzis, R., & McKee, A. (2002). *Primal leadership: Realizing the power of emotional intelligence.* Boston: Harvard Business School Press.

Huffman, J. B., & Hipp, K. K. (2004). *Reculturing schools as professional learning communities.* Lanham, MD: Scarecrow Education.

Merideth, E. M. (2007). *Leadership strategies for teachers* (2nd ed.). Thousand Oaks, CA: Corwin.

Wrap Up Your Reading With Reflection

When you have completed the series of group meetings or workshops on the chapters of *Failure Is Not an Option*, answer the following questions, and then take time as a group to celebrate your hard work and mastery of school-improvement theory and practice.

1. What is the most valuable lesson your school or district has learned from reading and discussing the book with your colleagues?
2. In light of what you have learned, what should be the two highest priority actions for improvement in your school or district?
3. What actions will you, individually or with colleagues, take as a result of what you have learned?
4. Sketch out a possible timeline for the actions you listed in answering questions 2 and 3.
5. What, if any, follow-up activities would you like your group to undertake?
6. What have you learned about collaboration and teamwork as a result of the activities and discussions in this guide?
    a. What did you like about this process?
    b. What would you do differently if you were to do this again?
7. Set a date to get back together to exchange what you've done. Identify how the group can help you as a result of your experience in applying this reading to your practice.

Resources

Resource 1. FNO Snapshot Rubric for Educational Leaders

District/School _____

Leader _____

Date _____

		Levels			
		One	*Two*	*Three*	*Four*
		• General understanding of principle's main concept • Can identify some possible actions and evidence that reflect principle	• Good understanding of expectations and processes needed for implementation • Clearly articulates the key elements and can identify reasonable range of actions and evidence, showing understanding	• In-depth understanding shown through actions aligned with desired outcomes • Is able to present a comprehensive range of evidence • Application is at conscious level	• Daily actions and decisions show internalized understanding of principle and focus on continuous improvement • Able to support colleagues, parents, and community in fostering the principle
Principles	Common mission, vision, values, and goals				
	Ensuring achievement for all students—systems for prevention and intervention				
	Collaborative teaming focused on teaching for learning				
	Data-based decisions for continuous improvement				
	Gaining active engagement from family and community				
	Building sustainable leadership capacity				

Resource 2. FNO Student-Success Model and Critical-Success Factors

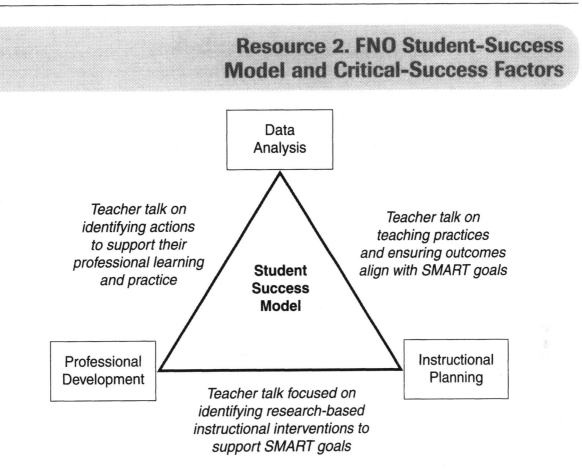

Data Analysis	Teachers analyze multiple sources of student data, such as standardized and publisher tests, formative assessments, student observation, and examining student work. Through this comprehensive study they determine a targeted priority for improvement and/or intervention.
Instructional Planning	Teachers identify the current instructional needs, based on the data analysis, and make an instructional plan to improve student performance. This plan is aimed at improving student achievement in the identified targeted priority.
Professional Development	Teachers determine the gap in their current repertoire to direct and support instruction aligned with the instructional priority. They use this information to build their professional development (PD) plan. Implementation of the PD plan includes monitoring student progress and making adaptations in the instructional process, based on student progress.

Source: Adapted with permission. *Triangulated Student Data to Inform Instruction* by Mary E. Dietz, 2002.

Resource 3. Williamston Zoomerang Survey: Tying Professional Development to Results

Zoomerang Survey Results

Grading for Learning

Response Status: Completes

Filter: No filter applied

Feb. 25, 2009, 9:21 AM PST

The content of this survey is based primarily on Ken O'Connor's (2007) book *A Repair Kit for Grading: 15 Fixes for Broken Grades.* Your help and time are greatly appreciated. The survey should take approximately 10 minutes.

1. In addition to academic achievement, I include student behaviors (effort, participation, adherence to classroom rules, etc.) in grades.		
Never	18	72%
Sometimes	4	16%
Almost always	2	8%
Always	1	4%
Total	25	100%
2. I reduce the student's grade/score on work submitted late.		
Never	20	80%
Sometimes	3	12%
Almost always	0	0%
Always	2	8%
Total	25	100%
3. I give points for extra credit or use bonus points.		
Never	12	48%
Sometimes	12	48%
Almost always	1	4%
Always	0	0%
Total	25	100%

4. I punish academic dishonesty (i.e., plagarism, cheating) with reduced grades or by assigning a zero.

Never	13	52%
Sometimes	8	32%
Almost always	3	12%
Always	1	4%
Total	25	100%

5. I consider attendance (excused and/or unexcused absences or tardies) in grade determination. For example, if a student is absent, fails to attend a performance, does not dress appropriately for class, or skips a class, she or he receives a lower grade or score.

Never	24	96%
Sometimes	1	4%
Almost always	0	0%
Always	0	0%
Total	25	100%

6. I include group scores (from collaborative group assignments) in grades.

Never	11	44%
Sometimes	12	48%
Almost always	2	8%
Always	0	0%
Total	25	100%

7. I organize information in my grading records by assessment methods (such as tests, quizzes, projects, and homework) or by summarizing the assessments into a single letter grade. (The opposite of this would be to organize and report evidence by standard or learning goals/GLCE—grade-level content expectations.)

Never	2	8%
Sometimes	1	4%
Almost always	7	28%
Always	15	60%
Total	25	100%

8. I determine and assign grades using letter-number relationships such as A = 93–100, A– = 90–92, B+ = 87–89, B = 83–86, B– = 80–82, etc. . . .

Never	2	8%
Sometimes	1	4%
Almost always	10	40%
Always	12	48%
Total	25	100%

(Continued)

(Continued)

9. I assign grades based on a student's achievement compared to other students. (The opposite of this would be to assign grades based on preset standards.)		
Never	19	76%
Sometimes	5	20%
Almost always	1	4%
Always	0	0%
Total	**25**	**100%**

10. In determining grades, I rely on evidence gathered using only quality assessments—assessments that have a clear purpose, clear learning goals, sound design, and avoidance of bias.		
Never	1	4%
Sometimes	2	8%
Almost always	16	64%
Always	6	24%
Total	**25**	**100%**

11. When assigning a final grade, I determine the grade by calculating the mean (average) of a series of scores. Moreover, I summarize the grade by strict mathematical calculation—nothing else is factored into the final grade.		
Never	3	12%
Sometimes	1	4%
Almost always	12	48%
Always	9	36%
Total	**25**	**100%**

12. I include zeros in grade determination when evidence is missing (such as if a student failed to turn in the assignment) or as a punishment (if a student cheated on an assignment).		
Never	7	28%
Sometimes	11	44%
Almost always	3	12%
Always	4	16%
Total	**25**	**100%**

13. I use evidence from formative assessments and practice to determine grades.		
Never	10	40%
Sometimes	8	32%
Almost always	4	16%
Always	3	12%
Total	**25**	**100%**

14. *I average or summarize all evidence gathered over time when reporting a final grade. (The opposite of this would be to allow new evidence to replace, not simply be added to, old evidence when determining a final grade. For example, if a student retakes a test, the new score would completely take the place of any old scores related to that skill.)*

Never	8	32%
Sometimes	6	24%
Almost always	6	24%
Always	5	20%
Total	**25**	**100%**

15. *I involve students in all stages of the assessment process and they understand from the onset how grades will be determined.*

Never	1	4%
Sometimes	6	24%
Almost always	10	40%
Always	8	32%
Total	**25**	**100%**

16. *I would like to use a standards-based report card in reporting grades.*

Yes, I am ready to rock and roll! Let's get moving.	8	32%
Yes, but I need a little bit more information on some concerns I have.	10	40%
Maybe, but I need more information and more time to digest.	7	28%
No, I disagree with this train of thought.	0	0%
Other, please specify.	0	0%

17. *If you expressed an interest in a standards-based report card, what would you need to make this happen? If you did not express an interest, please explain your reasoning and/or hesitation.*

[25 responses]

18. *I believe the primary purpose of grades is to*

Provide teachers with information for instructional planning.	1	4%
Provide information that students can use for self-evaluation.	3	12%
Communicate student achievement.	21	84%
Provide incentives to learn.	0	0%
Select, identify, or group students for certain educational paths or programs.	0	0%
Total	**25**	**100%**

(Continued)

(Continued)

19. I consistently use the "common special scores" symbols in my grade book and in communications with students and parents. Williamston Middle School's Common Special Scores: AB = Absent but needs to be made up EX = Excused and does not need to be made up Y = Assignment has been turned in MI = Missing NC = Not complete		
Never	0	0%
Sometimes	3	12%
Almost always	8	32%
Always	12	48%
Other, please specify		
20. Reflect upon your reading of the book How to Grade for Learning by Ken O'Connor. Please assign yourself a "grade" based on your reading progress.		
A = Completed the entire book	7	28%
B = Completed over 3/4 of the book	1	4%
C = Completed 1/2 of the book	3	12%
D = Completed 1/4 of the book	6	24%
F = Have not begun reading the book	8	32%
21. Think about the quality of discussion you have had with your grade-level content buddy on the content ("ah-ha moments" and "But, wait a minute, what about . . . ?") of the book How to Grade for Learning. What grade would you give yourself based on these discussions?		
A = Thorough and detailed discussions have occurred *and* been documented. We have exhausted the content.	0	0%
B = Thorough and detailed discussions (only) have occurred.	1	4%
C = We have had a few discussions with some depth, but need to make the time to continue them.	13	52%
D = We have had at least one discussion on the content.	6	24%
F = What?!?!? I was supposed to discuss something?!?!	5	20%
22. In the space provided, please share any additional information about grading for learning that you would like this team to consider in regards to building practices and/or the education of staff.		
[12 responses]		

Source: Used with permission from Christine Sermak.

Resource 4. FNO Tuning Protocol

What Are Tuning Protocols?

A *tuning protocol* is a staff-development process that is embedded in what a teacher does in the classroom. Or what an educator does in a school. A group of colleagues comes together to examine each other's work, honor the good things found in that work, and fine-tune it through a formal process of presentation and reflection (Lois Easton, 1999).

Tuning protocols provide a structure and process for professional dialogue to learn from our work. This process helps fine-*tune* educational practices using a *protocol* or formal process for examining our work in a supportive, problem-solving group.

Rationale

Four reasons to use tuning protocols are

1. *Tunings provide accountability beyond test scores.* We need to get different information from different kinds of data, not just comparisons against a population (norm-reference tests) or comparison to a standard (criterion-reference tests). We need a repertoire. We also need a source of data that is less invasive than a test.
2. *Tunings provide information useful in a classroom.* By looking directly at student work, we learn what students really know and can do in the context of their real work—and why. We also learn what students do not know and cannot do. These are important insights for anyone educating young people.
3. *Tunings build a learning community.* They are content rich since they focus on student work and educator practice. For these reasons, they ensure some level of application.
4. *Tunings work.*
   a. The process is relatively risk free. The protocol does not permit attack-counterattack, pro-con, offense-defense, or statement-rebuttal discourse.
   b. These results are richer than those from a typical discussion. Individuals who debate each other sidetrack the group and prevent deep conversations and discussions.
   c. Everybody learns from a tuning protocol. The tuning protocol allows everyone to think deeply about student work and educator practice, arrive at creative solutions, and connect with colleagues.

Source: Adapted from Lois Easton, *Powerful Designs for Professional Learning*, 2nd Ed., Dallas, TX: NSDC, 2008, pp. 239–240; Lois Easton, 1999, Tuning Protocols, *Journal of Staff Development*, 20(3), 55–56.

Setting Up the Tuning Protocol

Table Roles

Each team appoints the following:

- *Presenter.* The presenter brings the samples, sets the context, and describes the teaching/learning situation.
- *Table Facilitator.* The table facilitator ensures that participants stay on task, checks for "airtime" midway in the discussion, ensures appropriate, nonevaluative questions are asked.

- *Timekeeper.* The timekeeper ensures that time limits are kept for each section.
- *Feedback Monitor.* The feedback monitor checks for warm and cool feedback, making adjustment suggestions if needed, and ensures feedback is focused on the process and not a critique of the presenter.
- *Key Question Monitor.* The key question monitor observes the degree to which the key question is addressed, making adjustment suggestions if needed.

Norms for the Tuning Protocol Process

- Engage fully by asking questions and clarifying your thinking.
- Actively listen to understand the perspective of your colleagues.
- Manage your personal needs.

Tuning Protocol Assumptions

- We want to improve in our work as educators.
- We want to be kind, courteous, thoughtful, insightful, and provocative.
- We are "in this together." This is a collaborative process.

Step 1: Presenter Role

1. Presenter sets the context and describes the teaching/learning situation.
2. Participants listen and take notes without interrupting the presenter.
3. Participants are given time to examine their copy of the student work being discussed.
4. Chart the one or two key questions that the participants pose.

Key Questions

What do these pieces of student work tell us about the following?

- Instruction
- Design
- Strategies
- Decisions
- Personalization

Step 2: Clarifying Questions

1. Participants ask nonevaluative questions about the presentation. For example,
    - What happened before *X*?
    - What did you do next?
    - What did *Y* say?
2. Participants must guard against asking questions that approach evaluation. For example,
    - Why didn't you try *Z*?

Step 3: Individual Writing

1. Review the information and samples pertaining to warm and cool feedback.

2. Participants, including the presenter, write feedback comments about the presentation, addressing the key question or questions.

3. This part of the protocol helps each participant to focus on what to say during the participant discussion.

Step 4: Participant Discussion

1. Review the responsibilities of the table facilitator, feedback monitor, and key questions monitor.

2. Presenter remains completely silent while taking notes, perhaps turning away to avoid eye contact.

3. Participants describe or explain what is to be tuned and improved, with the presenter listening in.

4. Participants discuss the issues raised during the presentation to deepen their understanding of the situation and seek answers to the key questions.

5. Participants should strive for a balance of "warm" and "cool" feedback.

6. Participants should strive to contribute to substantive discourse.

Step 5: Presenter Reflection

1. Participants remain silent and take notes on the presenter reflection.

2. Presenter reflects aloud on the participants' discussion, using the issues raised to deepen understanding, considering possible answers to the questions posed.

3. Presenter projects about future actions, questions, and dilemmas.

Step 6: Debrief the Tuning Protocol

Plus/Delta Activity

- What worked well?
- What did you learn?
- How will you use this in your professional collaborations and instructional learning?
- How would you improve the engagement of participants in the tuning protocol?

Next Steps

Record three implications for instruction that came from the tuning protocol.

Closure

After the table has debriefed, the room facilitator thanks the presenters and table monitors for stepping forward in those roles.

Critical Aspects of Doing a Tuning on Your Own

Do's and Don'ts

☐ Tuning protocols work best if participants and presenters think of their work as a collaboration to help students learn.

❐ Be vigilant about keeping time. Be sure to work through the entire protocol for the process to be effective. Do not let one person monopolize any part of the protocol.

❐ Try to gather the same group each time a protocol is done.

❐ If presenters come from within a group of people who will, themselves, do a protocol, they'll feel a little less intimidated about sharing the work they and/or their students are doing.

❐ The group should be somewhat protective of the presenter—by making their work public, presenters expose themselves to a critique.

❐ The room facilitator should help participants recast or withdraw inappropriate comments. The room facilitator can also ask how "tough" the presenter wants participants to be.

❐ Participants should also be courteous, thoughtful, and provocative. Be provocative of substantive discourse. Many presenters may be used to blanket praise. Without thoughtful but probing cool questions and comments, they won't benefit from the tuning protocol experience. Presenters often say they'd have liked more cool feedback (Cushman, 1995).

❐ Consider having an outside facilitator who does not participate in the process, at least for the first tuning.

❐ The facilitator should make sure all steps are followed, keep time, be sure that the group acts according to the assumptions, monitor airtime, check for the balance of warm and cool feedback, and make sure the group addresses the presenter's key questions. Without a facilitator, consider having participants take on these roles.

● *Warm and Cool Feedback*

Joe McDonald, Coalition of Essential Schools, uses the terms *warm* and *cool feedback*. Nothing is gained if participants only praise, but praise should be part of a protocol: What worked? Nothing is gained if participants only criticize, but a critique should be part of a protocol: What would help students learn better?

- *Warm feedback* consists of statements that let the presenter know what is working. Warm feedback takes the form of praise for what seems effective.

- *Cool feedback* consists of statements or questions that help the presenter move forward. They are less criticism than a critique of the work. They are oriented to improving the work and the work context. Cool feedback is never about the presenter—only about what the presenter brought to be tuned. The best cool feedback occurs through "What if . . ." questions such as, "I wonder what would happen if . . ."

Resource 5. Williamston Graphic Organizer and Rubric for Writing

Sandwich Chart

Name _____ Date _____

Write your topic at the top. Add details to the middle layers. Add a concluding sentence at the bottom.

Topic:

Detail:

Detail:

Detail:

Concluding Sentence:

Paragraph Rubric

Name _____ Date _____

	4	3	2	1
Topic Sentence	The topic sentence thoughtfully and with engaging language states the main idea of the question or assigned topic.	The topic sentence clearly states the main idea of the question or assigned topic.	The topic sentence is unclear or weakly stated.	There is no topic sentence.
Supporting Details	The paragraph contains at least three sentences that support the main idea with reasons, details, or facts. The details demonstrate thoughtful reasoning and/or deep understanding.	The paragraph contains at least two or three supporting sentences, which demonstrate good reasoning and understanding of the topic.	The paragraph contains some details, but they demonstrate limited reasoning and understanding of the topic.	The paragraph contains inaccurate information or no supporting details.
Conclusion Sentence	A strong conclusion is developed, which effectively wraps up the paragraph and refers to the main idea without simply restating it.	The conclusion sentence wraps up the paragraph and refers to the main idea.	The conclusion is weak or unclear or simply repeats the introduction.	The paragraph lacks a conclusion.
Conventions of CUPS (Capitalization, Understanding, Punctuation, and Spelling)	The paragraph contains few, if any, CUPS errors.	The paragraph contains some CUPS errors, but they do not interfere with meaning.	The paragraph contains many CUPS errors that interfere with meaning.	An extreme lack of editing makes the paragraph challenging to read.

Source: Used with permission from Christine Sermak.

Resource 6. Williamston Professional Development Agenda

Williamston Middle School

We will be advocates for all learners, all of the time.

6 Principles of High-Performing Schools/Hope Foundation

☐ Common, shared mission, vision, values, and goals
☑ Ensuring achievement for ALL students
☑ Collaborative teaming focused on teaching and learning
☑ Using data to guide decision making and continuous improvement
☐ Gaining active engagement from family and community
☐ Building sustainable leadership capacity

● *Inservice/Professional Development Agenda (Full Day)*

Location: Williamston Middle School Media Center

Who: All Staff

Date: Wednesday, November 26, 2008, from 7:30 a.m. to 2:00 p.m. **(note time change)**

● *By the conclusion of this meeting, we will have discussed*

Strategies that are needed to achieve our

- *Courageous Leadership Academy SMART Goal.* "We will increase common practices that support students and one another."
- *Building School Improvement Goal.* "Students will be proficient readers and *writers* in all content areas."

Specifically,

- *Planner Usage.* Strategies to increase relevancy, implementation, and parent support
- *Students Will Be Able to . . . (SWBAT).* Expectations and why
- *Walk-Throughs.* What are they; their benefits; sign up to visit colleague's classroom
- *Writing.* Data, next steps (expand repertoire of writing strategies with an emphasis on organization and editing)

Time	What	Who
7:30 a.m.	• Collection of intellikeys • Welcome and overview of day • Hornet distribution (2)	Tania
7:40–7:55 a.m.	• Why are we here? What is our call? • Why are *all* of us needed in this process? ○ Survey using clickers • View video from Dallas ISD (8 min.) http://www.webertube.com/mediadetails.php?key=fb8f1eda792ae6471f8f	Christine

7:55–8:10 a.m.	• "We will increase common practices that support students and one another."
	  ○ Planner usage
	  ○ SWBAT (students will be able to . . .)
	  ○ Walk-throughs
		Anne, Katy, Laura, Tania, Tim, and Steve

8:10–9:30 a.m.	• "Students will be proficient *writers* in all content areas."
	  ○ Why focus on this and not other initiates?
	  ○ *Solutions.* How do we use intervention and curriculum contact time (ICC) with common assessment work?
	
	• English language arts historical perspective
	
	• What teaching and assessing of reading and writing are you currently doing in your classroom?
	
	• A closer look at data (where is *our* writing focus?)
	• Why is writing in *all* classes important?
		Christine
		
		Narda
		
		Christine, all (individual reflection), teacher sharing
		
		Tammy
		All, Kelly

Break (10 minutes)		
9:40–11:00 a.m.	• What can we do to get students to write more (expanding our repertoire of writing activities)? ○ *Action.* Groups (read, discuss, present)	Kelly
Lunch and Comedy Break (Brought to you by Williamston Middle School Full Force Factor) (30 minutes)—Provided by WMS in Cafeteria		
11:30 a.m.–12:30 p.m.	• *Writing Prompt.* What is your favorite Thanksgiving memory? Or, what are your plans for tomorrow? ○ *Focus Correction Areas (FCA).* Writing to topic, use of details	Deb

Time	What	Who
	• How can we teach the writing and editing processes using common language? ○ *Action.* Graphic organizers and paragraph response with FCA ○ "Hamburger" activity ○ CUPS (capitalization, understanding, punctuation, and spelling) activity	Deb, all Deb Sandy
12:30– 2:00 p.m.	• How will this look at the grade-level content area? How does this fit with my common assessment work? ○ *Action.* Work period with department buddy; choose writing-to-learn activity, take to next level (i.e., written response), FCA	Christine Grade-level content-area buddies Special education team elective course team
Snacks and Beverages Provided in Media Center		
2:00 p.m.	• Submit plan to Sermak with loose implementation timeline • Personal reflection on professional development (PD) day • Due by end of second quarter: student writing samples to Sermak (electronically)	All

Source: Used with permission from Christine Sermak.

Resource 7. Strategies for Making Time

☐ Share classrooms. Plan and schedule team teaching and multidisciplinary class time.

☐ Adjust daily schedule. Teachers agree to arrive sufficiently in advance of classes starting to allow for meeting time. Classes can also be started late one day a week to add 15 to 20 extra minutes to regular early meeting time.

☐ Bring classes together. Have classes exchange visits on a reciprocal basis (e.g., fifth graders visit first-grade classes to read or work with younger children, and first graders visit fifth graders on alternate weeks) and be supervised by one teacher, freeing up the other one.

☐ Use assemblies to free up time. Schedule buildingwide or schoolwide events (movies, assemblies, and so on) during which classroom teachers can meet while students are supervised by counselors, paraprofessionals, or administrators.

☐ Give common assignments. Several classrooms of students at the same grade level (or taking the same course) are given the same assignment or project simultaneously. Videos, library time, or other related activities are scheduled for all the classes at once, freeing their teachers to meet together while aides, volunteers, or others supervise.

☐ Use parent or business volunteers. Involve parents as aides or chaperones for appropriate activities. Invite local business representatives to share their particular expertise as they supervise classes.

☐ Free up the fifth day. Schedule all academic classes to take place four days each week, leaving the fifth day free for team meetings while students rotate to art, music, PE, technology, the library, and so on.

☐ Reduce the number of all-staff meetings, and replace them with smaller team meetings where the topics under discussion can be tailored to the needs of the group (Pardini, 1999).

☐ Use paraprofessionals, student teachers, and aides to cover classes on a regular basis.

☐ Allocate more staff positions to classroom teaching than to pullout teaching and/or support roles (Darling-Hammond, 1999).

☐ Implement schedules that engage students with fewer teachers each day for longer periods of time (Darling-Hammond, 1999).

☐ Free teachers from nonprofessional activities (e.g., playground, bus duty, and so on).

☐ Use professional development funding and time allocation for teamwork.

Resource 8. Self-Assessment

Do the Cultural Norms of Your School Promote School Improvement?

	Never	Rarely	Sometimes	Often	Always
1. *Shared goals.* "We know where we are going."	1	2	3	4	5
2. *Responsibility for success.* "We must succeed."	1	2	3	4	5
3. *Collegiality.* "We're working on it together."	1	2	3	4	5
4. *Continuous improvement.* "We can get better."	1	2	3	4	5
5. *Lifelong learning.* "Learning is for everyone."	1	2	3	4	5
6. *Risk taking.* "We learn by trying something new."	1	2	3	4	5
7. *Support.* "There's always someone there to help."	1	2	3	4	5
8. *Mutual support.* "Everyone has something to offer."	1	2	3	4	5
9. *Openness.* "We can discuss our differences."	1	2	3	4	5
10. *Celebration and humor.* "We feel good about ourselves."	1	2	3	4	5

Add the 4s and 5s

Source: Adapted from *Changing Our Schools*, 1996, by Louise Stoll and Dean Fink.

How Effective Is Your School?

	Never	*Rarely*	*Sometimes*	*Often*	*Always*
1. *Instructional leadership* (firm and purposeful, a participative approach, the leading professional)	1	2	3	4	5
2. *Shared vision and clear goals* (unity of purpose, consistency of practice)	1	2	3	4	5
3. *Shared values and beliefs*	1	2	3	4	5
4. *A learning environment* (an orderly atmosphere, an attractive working environment)	1	2	3	4	5
5. *Teaching and curriculum focus* (maximization of learning time, academic emphasis, focus on achievement)	1	2	3	4	5
6. *High expectations* (for all, communications of expectations, intellectual challenge for all)	1	2	3	4	5
7. *Positive student behavior* (clear and fair discipline and feedback)	1	2	3	4	5
8. *Frequent monitoring of student progress* (ongoing monitoring, evaluating school performance)	1	2	3	4	5
9. *Student involvement and responsibility* (high student self-esteem, positions of responsibility, control of work)	1	2	3	4	5
10. *Climate for learning* (positive physical environment, recognition, incentives)	1	2	3	4	5

Source: Adapted from Halton Board of Education (1988). Used with permission.

School Typology

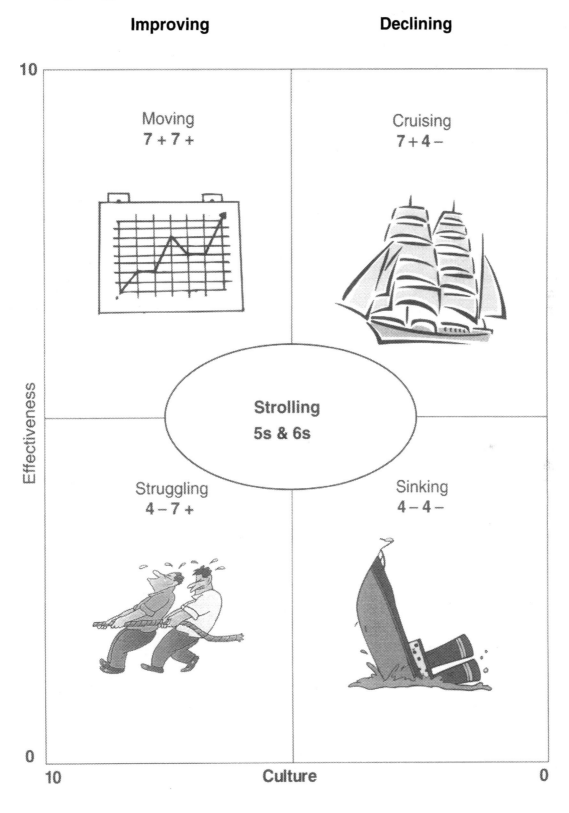

Source: Adapted from *Changing Our Schools*, 1996, by Louise Stoll and Dean Fink.

Three Strategies of School Development

III. Good Schools →	II. Moderately Effective Schools →	I. Failing Schools →
Keeping good schools effective and stimulated Becoming more effective		
✓ Build capacity ✓ Focus on teaching and learning ✓ Mainly work with existing leadership and support ✓ Some outside pressure/support ✓ Larger lesson periods to promote classroom creativity ✓ Broaden teacher leadership ✓ Listen and respond to students ✓ Motivate disillusioned staff ✓ Staff focused on purposes	✓ Extensive intervention and support ✓ Usually new leadership ✓ Target priorities for visible improvement, i.e., dress codes, attendance ✓ Building teacher competence and confidence in teaching strategies	✓ External partnerships ✓ Access to networks ✓ Exposure to new ideas/practices ✓ Consolidating collaboration ✓ Celebrating success ✓ Minimal external pressure

Source: David Hopkins, *School Improvement for Real* (2001). New York: Routledge/Falmer. Used with permission from Thomson Publishing Services.

Resource 9. Strategies for Dealing With Resistance

When faced with resistance, most people feel challenged. They feel that they must overcome the resistance in order to win their point. This instinct to overcome can actually lead to counterproductive behaviors. Some of these ineffective behaviors include

- *Use of Power.* Meeting force with force to overcome the resistance
- *Manipulating Those Who Oppose.* Finding subtle ways to apply pressure, or giving false impressions or partial information
- *Applying Force of Reason.* Overwhelming opponents with facts, figures, and flowcharts
- *Ignoring the Resistance.* Failing to address it in the hopes that it will go away on its own
- *Playing off Relationships.* Using friendships as leverage to get others to agree
- *Making Deals.* Offering something in exchange for agreement (e.g., trade-offs)
- *Killing the Messenger.* Getting rid of or bypassing the resistor
- *Giving In Too Soon.* Ceding your position before exploring the true level of resistance or the possibility of common understanding (Ontario Institute for Studies in Education at University of Toronto, 2001)

According to research from the University of Toronto, these common responses actually increase people's resistance. Even if they are effective in the short term, the win may not be worth the long-term costs of sabotage, compliance versus commitment, or people opting out of the implementation phase.

We can better deal with resistance by remembering a set of core behaviors, or touchstones. As we develop strategies for dealing with resistors, each strategy should be consistent with these touchstones:

- *Maintain Clear Focus.* Don't let the fog of resistance obscure your vision of your original goal. Yet, while never losing sight of the long-range goal, you must also keep an eye on the work of the moment. By maintaining a clear focus, you can switch your attention back and forth between what is going on at the moment and what you are ultimately trying to accomplish.
- *Embrace Resistance.* Although it may seem counterintuitive, resistance can actually serve a positive purpose in your efforts to build consensus. If you are to overcome objections, you must know what they *are*—and resistance provides you with that information.
- *Respect Those Who Resist.* Listen to what your resistors have to say with an open mind; do not automatically assume that they are uninformed, unjustified, or motivated purely by self-interest. Treat them with respect and dignity and be completely truthful.
- *Relax.* When someone pushes against us, it is instinctive for us to push back. It is that instinct, however, that prevents us from relaxing and embracing resistance. By relaxing—and not pushing back—you can allow your resistors to talk and tell you their thoughts. And once you understand their thoughts, you can use them to begin seeking common ground.
- *Join With the Resistance.* By listening with an open mind and exploring the ideas of the resistors, you can begin to identify areas you have in common. Building support for your idea happens when you find this common ground—this merging of interests and concerns.

Source: Adapted from *Dealing With Resistance,* OISE/UT (2001). To read more about this topic, see Rick Maurer's (1996) *Beyond the Wall of Resistance: Unconventional Strategies That Build Support for Change.*

Resource 10. Running River Elementary School Mission Statement

The mission of Running River Elementary School is to provide an opportunity for every student to master grade-level skills regardless of previous academic performance, family background, socioeconomic status, race, or gender. It is our purpose to educate all students to high levels of academic performance, while fostering positive growth in social/emotional behaviors and attitudes. The entire staff pledges itself to these student outcomes.

Resource 11. Development Process for Mission, Vision, Values, and Goals

The first step in the collaborative process of developing your school's mission, vision, values, and goals is identifying the underlying beliefs and priorities of all stakeholders and seeing what personal obstacles may prevent them from acting on those beliefs. The steps below will help you begin developing the four pillars of your own professional learning community.

Developing the Mission

The development of a mission statement should be the first step in the mission, vision, values, and goals axiom. As soon as a leadership team is formed, a timeline should be developed with "no later than" dates entered for each activity below. The process should begin early in the school year, and it should take three to four months to complete. In a two-semester year, you may want to try to complete the mission development by the end of the first semester.

The process is as follows.

● *Plan the Questioning, Drafting,*
   Review, and Adoption Process

Planning the process that leads to the adoption of the mission statement is the job of the leadership team, or a task force composed of some of its members, under the supervision of the principal. They should draw up a written plan for developing the mission statement that includes ample time for the crucial first step—questioning, discussion, and debate. The plan should include timelines for each step and should ensure that all constituencies of the school community have an opportunity to review the draft and participate in the approval process.

● *Review and Critique Your Existing Statement*
   and Examine Current Attitudes and Beliefs

The first step in drafting a mission statement is to involve all school staff—and parents and students as appropriate—in a serious and ongoing dialogue about the purpose of the school and the responsibility of educators. The principal and members of the leadership team facilitate the dialogue so that all voices receive a respectful hearing. All participants should ask themselves and each other the three essential questions about the school's mission, and all stakeholders should have a chance to enter the debate. Ultimately, the goal of the discussion is to reach a consensus about the answers to each of the three questions.

At many schools, there may be broad agreement that the answer to the first question, "What do we expect students to learn?" is "To become contributing members of society," "To become lifelong learners," or "To realize their full potential." It may require considerable discussion, however, to lead members of the community to a consensus that schools were founded and continue to exist to teach academic and social skills, that many standards for expected achievement levels exist, and that schools are mandated by society to help students reach these levels. There is likely to be even greater debate over the next two questions, which require participants to examine their attitudes about various kinds of assessments, their expectations for their students, and their attitudes toward their own ability and responsibility to turn around student failure.

Because these issues are so contentious, it may be necessary to continue the period of discussion and debate for several weeks or even a couple of months. During this period, however, the leadership team should begin drafting possible mission statements. These drafts can become focuses for the ongoing debate. The principal and members of the leadership team should facilitate the discussion, which can take place in open meetings, focus groups, interviews, and through the use of surveys and questionnaires.

● *Draft the Statement*

Although the actual drafting of the mission statement can be done by a small (two- to three-person) task force, members of the leadership team should be actively involved in each stage of the process. They should discuss the views articulated during the questioning and discussion activities and decide on desirable content and language before anything is written.

● *Submit the Draft for Review by All Appropriate*
Stakeholders and Revise It in Accordance With Their Suggestions

The draft document should first be submitted to all members of the faculty. When their comments and suggestions have been incorporated, the revised document can be submitted to students and families for comment. After reviewing responses and making any necessary revisions, the final version should be prepared for approval by all stakeholders.

● *Adopt and Disseminate the Mission Statement*

The final draft of the mission statement should first be submitted to the faculty as a whole for approval and adoption. The principal or another school leader should impress upon staff that the statement is not just words on a piece of paper; it is a solemn commitment of the entire school community to develop an organizational culture dedicated to high-quality student learning. It is only fair to point out that carrying out the mission will require many changes in the way things are done in the school.

After the faculty have adopted the mission statement, it should be presented to the parent group, older students, and the central administration for approval. After all stakeholders have approved the statement, it should be widely publicized and disseminated— posted on corridor walls, included in newsletters or bulletins, perhaps even posted in each classroom. As soon as possible, it should be incorporated into the school's letterhead, Web site, and any other visible face of the school.

Developing the Vision

As soon as the leadership team is formed, a timeline should be developed with "no later than" dates entered for each activity listed here.

In a two-semester year, an attempt could be made to complete work on the vision statement by the end of the first semester. Work on the vision statement will be concurrent with the development of the school profile and either concurrent with or lagging only slightly behind work on the mission statement. The steps for developing a vision are

- ### 1. Plan to Gather Views About a Vision of the School's Future and to Develop the Vision Document

This should be the job of the principal and the leadership team. The plan should include sufficient time for engaging all members of the school community in a dialogue about what the school can and should be—what the end result of the improvement process should look like. This step may involve developing surveys or questionnaires or planning meetings and focus groups. In many cases, these activities can be combined with those that focus on the school's mission.

- ### 2. Seek Dialogue and Ideas From All Staff and School Community Representatives

Initiating and maintaining a continuing conversation about improving the school is one of the most effective strategies for changing the school's climate. The dialogue can be conducted by the principal or by members of the leadership team. The means may include small meetings and focus groups, surveys and questionnaires, and a series of one-on-one conversations between members of the leadership team and representatives of various constituencies in the school community. In many cases, combinations of all these methods are used.

Even when formal meetings or by-appointment conversations are completed, the talk is likely to continue—and it can be a valuable way to encourage the collegiality and collaboration that is the basis of an effective school. The principal and leadership team, as a whole, should be closely involved in deciding what kinds of questions or topics should be explored by various constituencies, but a small task force is adequate to collect opinions and draft the document.

- ### 3. Draft the Vision Statement, and Submit It for Review, Revision, and Adoption by Stakeholders

As noted earlier, in many schools the vision document contains several different sections. These may refer to topics such as curriculum or school climate, or they may refer to groups, such as teaching staff or students. The leadership team decides on the topics for each section of the document. The team may decide to form several task forces, each working on one section, and then all come together to combine the separate sections into a complete document. Alternatively, they may undertake to have a single small group draft the entire document. Whatever method is chosen, the principal and leadership team should review all the sections and merge them into a single document.

- ### 4. Communicate the Adopted Vision Statement

After adoption, the vision statement should be communicated to the entire learning community and should be present as a constant reminder of what the school aims to become. The lead sentences of each section, for example, could be inscribed on a poster placed in a central location.

Developing the Values Statement

Begin working on a statement of values as your work on the mission and vision winds up. In a two-semester school, the work on the values statement should begin early in the second semester. Work on the values statement may be concurrent with the development of the goals statement and should occur in a context of awareness of the disaggregated data and information gathered in the school profile. The steps for developing the statement of values are

● *1. Develop a Plan for Having Each Role Group in the School Community Draft, Revise, and Adopt a Values Statement*

The principal and leadership team should work together to decide which groups should contribute statements of their values to the document. Normally, the groups would include administrators, teaching staff, support staff, parents, and students. A plan should be drawn up that includes the designation of task forces or leaders within each group and a timeline for discussion and consensus building, drafting, review, revision, and group approval followed by discussion, review, and adoption of the composite document by all stakeholders.

● *2. Have Each Group Draft, Review, and Approve Its Part of the Statement*

Each group (or representative task force of each group) should review the school's mission and vision statements, then discuss and list the kinds of behaviors and attitudes that can move the school toward the articulated vision. Leaders of each task force should ensure that all members of the constituent group participate in focus groups or brainstorming sessions to help identify the values to be listed.

Examining current assumptions and expectations is the first step in affirming new values based on the belief that all children can perform at a high standard of learning when taught by committed teachers utilizing the best possible instructional practices. Teachers may be willing to commit themselves, in their daily work, to the responsibility of seeing that every child is learning—but unless they truly believe that the child *can* learn and that their teaching can help him or her do so, they will quickly burn out. The corollary to an expressed belief in children's potential for learning is recognition and acceptance of the teachers' primary professional responsibility: to make learning happen. Acceptance of this responsibility should be central to the faculty's values statement, and the values statements of other groups should include a similar recognition of their role and an expression of responsibility to support their efforts.

● *3. Have All Stakeholders Review, Revise, and Adopt the Combined Statements*

As task forces from each group complete a draft of the values statement, the group as a whole should have the chance to review them and offer comments and suggestions. All groups should be reminded that the values expressed must be consistent with the mission statement and should provide a basis for the vision. In other words, reviewers should ask about each articulated value, "If we behave this way, will our school look more like the ideal we described in our vision statement?" If the answer is no, the value should be revised.

The principal and the leadership team should decide on the best venues and times to distribute the completed, composite values statement to all stakeholder representatives and to collect comments. Representatives of each constituent group should work with the principal to decide on the most appropriate times and means for seeking adoption of the values statements.

4. Disseminate and Communicate the Values Statement Throughout the Learning Community

The principal, assisted by the process coach, should ensure that the values statement is disseminated throughout the learning community and that the values expressed are communicated frequently and clearly at every opportunity. For example, suppose a particular school's statement included a commitment in the students' section to "work hard to take advantage of the learning opportunities offered to us," and the teachers' values included the statement "We will use our knowledge and expertise to support student learning and remove impediments to continuing progress."

A parent, enrolling her son in this school, might say, "He works hard, but he can't seem to make much progress in math—he just doesn't seem to understand it." An appropriate response from the counselor might be, "We value hard work, but we want to make sure it's productive. Our staff is committed to seeing that students progress, so we'll find ways to help him overcome his problems with math."

Developing Goals

Before a final goals statement can be adopted, teams must have the school profile on hand as well as a large amount of disaggregated data and copies of the mission and vision statements. Schools may find, however, that the adoption of interim goals early in the year can provide direction and impetus to the improvement process. The leadership team and principal should decide, early in the year, on a timetable and plan for developing both interim and long-term goals.

Develop a Plan for Drafting, Revising, and Adopting a Goals Statement

Interim goals, adopted early in the year, may be developed by the principal and the leadership team and presented to the faculty for discussion and review. Such interim goals would be short term, limited to priority improvements that can be implemented fairly quickly, and put in place well before the end of the school year.

A more comprehensive set of short- and long-term goals requires more time and thoughtful analysis of data, establishment of priorities, review, revision, and development of consensus about what is necessary and possible. Under the direction of the principal, the leadership team should create a plan that provides for review of data, an assessment of available resources, sufficient discussion and review by those most affected—the teachers—and an established and consistent means of monitoring progress.

Analyze data as a foundation for establishing priorities and setting realistic goals. Only reliable, up-to-date, carefully disaggregated data can provide teams with the information and direction they need to establish priorities and decide what targets are realistic in the short and long term. Much data may already have been included in the school profile. Other necessary data, particularly the performance outcomes of identified subgroups in core curricular subjects, should be fully available and shared among task force and leadership team members. Priorities should reflect hard evidence pointing to areas with the greatest problems. In reviewing data, teams should take note of the assessments used to provide the outcomes they are analyzing and consider specifying their continuing use for monitoring progress. The suggested priorities and goals should be accompanied by a list of assessments deemed most useful and revelatory for gauging learning outcomes.

● *Have All Grade-Level Subject-Area Staff Discuss, Refine, Limit, and Prioritize Suggested Goals*

The burden of meeting any adopted goal target will fall largely on teaching staff in the area of focus. Such staff should be consulted early in the goal-setting process. They should be able to review all available data and encouraged to comment on the practicality and realism of proposed targets.

● *Draw Up a Draft Goal Statement and Submit It for Review, Revision, and Adoption*

This activity involves a lot of hard choices, and members of the leadership team may have differing but passionately held views on where the school's primary improvement efforts should be focused. The principal may need to exercise considerable leadership and management skills to help the team reach consensus. Although the mission, vision, and values statements involved all stakeholders in a direct and personal way, the goals statement, if it focuses as it should on academic skills and outcomes, has the greatest effect on the teaching staff. Consequently, teachers should have the largest opportunity to review and comment on the developing document. Administrators should respond to the teachers' suggestions and comments with thoughtfulness and respect, but they should not let a faculty member's fear of higher standards or a changed climate turn them aside from insisting on high expectations for progress and improvement.

● *Develop a Plan for Monitoring Progress Toward Goals*

A goal statement that is adopted and ignored will not move a school one inch nearer its improvement targets. Progress—defined by outcomes on selected assessments—must be monitored regularly, consistently, and frequently. A plan for doing so must be a part of the goals statement and must be adopted simultaneously with the goals themselves.

Such a plan should state at what intervals progress is to be measured, the instruments to be used, and the amount of progress deemed acceptable at each occasion. Although state achievement tests may be the monitoring instrument of most interest to the state and the public, the outcomes tend to be too delayed and too late for prompt corrective action. Schools must have other assessments that are easily administered and scored, that are relevant to what is being taught in the classrooms at the time, and that provide more immediate feedback. Ideally, schools will choose to use a combination of objective tests and performance assessments. Whatever monitoring plan is adopted, it should provide for revision of interim goals or modifications of teaching strategies whenever outcomes indicate a change is necessary.

Resource 12. Worksheet for Developing a School Improvement Plan

Work either singly or in small groups to answer the following questions.

1. List all prevention and intervention strategies already in place at your school, grouping them in the following categories, which correspond to the ones in the pyramid below.
   a. Strategies for identified underachievers (entering ninth graders)
   b. Strategies for all ninth graders
   c. Strategies for persistent underachievers
   d. Strategies for fewer than 5% of underachievers

2. Evaluate each strategy carefully to determine whether it fits with your school's philosophical structure (i.e., mission, vision, values, and goals).
   a. Place a check mark beside those that are already philosophically sound and do not need to be changed.
   b. Place a C beside those strategies that will need to be modified to better fit into your school's philosophical structure.

3. Now, looking at your pyramid of interventions as a whole, identify any gaps in the structure that need to be filled (e.g., strategies to support specific subgroups). Add those strategies to your earlier list in question 1, placing an N beside them to mark them as new.

Adlai Stevenson High School Pyramid of Interventions

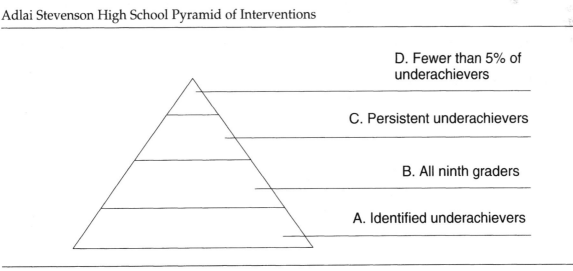

Source: Failure Is Not an Option video series (2002).

Resource 13. Pyramid of Support at Coyote Ridge Elementary School

Purpose

To identify additional support systems at varying levels of intensity in order for students to perform at their academic and/or behavioral potential.

Green Level: No Additional Support Needed

Student is achieving at the desired level.

Yellow Level: Least Intensive

● *Individual Teacher*

- Look at prior records and assessment information to determine student strengths and areas of need
- Converse informally with prior teachers
- Conference formally with parents two times per year
- Contact parents for additional conferences
- Provide midterm grades if below a C (depending on grade level)
- Provide additional reports to parents if student is failing
- Use classroom or grade-level volunteers to tutor small groups or individual students
- Continually assess students for movement in levels, for example, running records, district reading assessment, phonological awareness literacy service, basic reading inventory, math boxes, writing rubrics
- Complete and implement a literacy achievement plan
- Meet with administrator for support and suggestions
- Meet with specialists (PE, music, art, technology, teacher librarian) for support and suggestions
- Consult and set observations with special education specialists
- Use "buddy system" within classroom
- Use second-step curriculum
- Implement informal articulation therapy for speech
- Use informal occupational therapy and physical therapy strategies
- Establish consistent building rules and expectations that carry over into classroom expectations—taught, reinforced, posted
- Use classroom "contracts for success"
- Reinforce using classroom and buildingwide recognition, for example, Coyote of the Month, Coyote Howl Postcards, Positive Office Referrals
- Implementation of Coyote Ridge 3 (positive behavioral system) throughout the building

● *Grade Level*

- Use groups within the school day based on academic need (reconfigure groups of students based on need between classes)

- Identify specific skills and concepts based on data from unit tests and reconfigure groups of students for review and reteaching activities
- Use district coaches, building student achievement coach, or gifted and talented coordinator to model lessons or help plan lessons using differentiation strategies
- Complete classroom data forms for identification of students not performing at level; discuss with administrator

Orange Level: More Intensive

Receive yellow support and consider the following:

Cross-Grade-Level, Specialist, and Volunteer Support

- Utilize special education staff to supplement (not supplant) instruction through best practices (e.g., multisensory)
- Provide math club for those struggling with basic concepts (Grades 3 and 4)
- Provide opportunities for students to move to an appropriate grade level for matched instruction (i.e., fourth grade to second, kindergarten to first)
- Utilize trained volunteers to support small-groups or individuals in a variety of content areas
- Utilize literacy coordinator or interventionist for small-group instruction using best practices such as Success Oriented Achievement Realized (SOAR) or Dynamic Indicators of Basic Early Literacy Skills (DIBELS).
- Provide or support summer school or tutoring opportunities
- See counselor on short-term basis
- Participate in *Learning Together* peer tutoring reading program, Grades 2 through 4 and 3 through 5
- Other:
  - Bubble Groups (those 10 points above or below cut scores) before or after school on state testing
  - Homework Club before or after school
  - College/high school students tutor additional groups or individuals
  - Individualized education plan less than 21% of the time out of the classroom

Red Level: Most Intensive

Provide yellow and orange support and consider the following:

Mentor System

- Provide short-term one-on-one counseling with school social worker or psychologist
- Implement intensive behavior support plans based on functional behavioral assessment
- Implement one-on-one intervention/enrichment
- Use student/staff member buddy system where the student meets with the staff member weekly to check on student progress
- Student may be referred to special education team for consideration for testing
- Collaboration with outside therapists/medical personnel

- Other:
  - Individualized education program (IEP) more than 21% of the time out of the classroom

Note: Special education, English language learners, gifted and talented, Section 504, and significant support needs students may be at any color on the Pyramid of Support based on the identified and implemented support being provided.

Consider the following for students on an IEP when placing them on the pyramid:

- Hours of support on IEP (certified and classified staff)
- Number of providers
- Outside support (family therapy, outside speech/language, vision therapy)
- Formal behavior plan
- Medical needs (identified by a doctor)

Source: Used with permission of Kari Cocozzella.

Resource 14. Developing a System of Prevention and Intervention

Begin the process by working with your colleagues to sketch plans or procedures on separate sheets of paper for (1) identifying students in need of extra support and attention; (2) monitoring such students intensively; (3) providing mentors, "good friends," or other adult support to these students; and (4) establishing intervention programs. List programs that already exist and note whether they need to be modified or expanded and, if so, in what ways. For new programs, state the specific goal and then address the following questions.

1. Identification

- What criteria, data, or information will we use to identify incoming students who need extra attention?
- Who will be responsible for gathering and evaluating this information?
- When will this be done?
- What obstacles need to be confronted?

2. Monitoring

- What kinds of ongoing information or data about identified students will be collected?
- How often will the information be gathered?
- What will be the vehicle for entering and transmitting the information?
- Who will be asked to provide it?
- Who will gather and evaluate it?
- How promptly will it be reviewed?
- What obstacles need to be confronted?
- What are some strategies for overcoming these obstacles?

3. Mentoring

- What kind of mentoring program is needed in our school?
- How can we ensure that every identified student has a "best friend" adult?
- Who should be recruited to fill such roles? Certified personnel only? Clerical staff? Custodial staff? Kitchen workers? Parents and community volunteers? Also, what guidelines, orientation, or training should be provided to them?
- Who should provide or lead the training?
- What should be the procedure for pairing students with mentors? Should meetings between students and mentors be structured or allowed to develop naturally?
- What communication tree should exist for mentors who become aware of problems?
- What obstacles need to be confronted?
- What are some strategies for overcoming these obstacles?

4. Intervention

- What is a reasonable and specific goal for each prevention or improvement program that we plan to implement?
- What resources are available for such programs (money, personnel, space, time, and so on)?
- What criteria should be established for selecting students for the programs?
- Should the program be mandatory or optional?
- What benchmark or standard do we hope to meet with each intervention, and what assessment and evaluation data will determine the program's success?
- How often will each intervention program be evaluated?
- What obstacles need to be confronted?
- What are some strategies for overcoming these?

Resource 15. Instructional Learning Walks

Focus Principles

Principle 1. Common mission, vision, values, and goals

Principle 2. Ensuring achievement for *all* students; systems for prevention and intervention

Principle 3. Collaborative teaming focused on teaching and learning

Principle 4. Using data to guide decision making and continuous improvement

Principle 5. Gaining active engagement from family and community

Principle 6. Building sustainable leadership capacity

Objectives for This Session

Participants will

1. Build a shared understanding of quality instruction through the process of defining indicators of quality instruction.
2. Learn to define, describe, and identify indicators of quality instruction through the instructional learning-walk process.
3. Learn what quality instruction looks like and how it contributes to student success.

Agenda

1. Welcome and introductions
2. Instructional learning walks: Steps 1 through 7
3. Plus/delta and next steps
4. HOPE evaluation
5. Closure

Group Norms

HOPE's Meeting Norms	Seven Norms of Collaboration
• Everyone has the right to be heard • Ideas, thoughts, and suggestions are generated with positive intentions • Starting and ending times are honored • Side conversations are avoided • Everyone focuses on group work and directions • Cell phones are on vibrate	• Pausing • Paraphrasing • Probing for specificity • Putting ideas on the table • Paying attention to self and others • Presuming positive intentions • Practicing a balance of inquiry and advocacy

Purpose

Instructional learning walks contribute to building shared understanding of quality instruction within the professional learning community through the process of defining indicators of quality instruction. The *instructional learning walk* process helps define, describe, and identify indicators of quality instruction. Learning what quality instruction looks like and including these practices contribute to student success.

Engaging in *instructional learning walks* is a professional development activity. Observing and defining indicators of quality instruction helps the work of developing a professional community by engaging in identifying the existence and frequency of the indicators of quality instruction. The classroom, name of teacher, and specific students are not important to the task.

Step 1: Brainstorm a List of Observable Indicators of Quality Instruction

1. Think of a lesson you have taught or observed that was highly successful in terms of participation and outcomes.
2. Think of these categories: teacher behaviors, student behaviors, and other indicators.
3. What were some of the key attributes of the lesson that contributed to its success in each category?
4. Individually, list teacher behaviors, student behaviors, and other indicators that you expect to see when quality instruction is present.

Step 2: Norm the Indicators of Quality Instruction as a Group

1. In teams or small groups, share your individual lists.
2. Combine and refine the lists to form one comprehensive list.
3. Continue combining and refining until you have a list of three to five indicators in each category (teacher behaviors, student behaviors, other indicators).

Some examples of possible indicators are student engagement, exploring students' ideas, thinking or reflection time, inquiry, and clear student expectations.

Step 3: Check Indicators of Quality Instruction

Be sure you have distinguished between indicators of quality instruction and lesson design and instructional strategies. For example, an indicator might be "student engagement" while one strategy the teacher is using to achieve engagement might be "cooperative learning."

Note: The research-based strategies from *Classroom Instruction That Works: Researched-Based Strategies for Increasing Student Achievement* (Marzano, Pickering, & Pollock, 2001) explain a number of strategies that have been proven to make a difference in student learning. Your lists should not include specific strategies as such, but rather should be what you can agree on as useful for describing and identifying effective instruction.

Step 4: Check for Understanding by Describing Each Indicator of Quality Instruction

Each indicator should have a description so that when looking for quality instruction, no one is confused regarding "what to look for."

When describing indicators of quality instruction, use observational language. What does each indicator look and sound like?

Examples of Indicator Descriptions of Student Engagement

- The student is encouraged to participate and express ideas.
- The student is seeking to understand and asks questions.

Examples of Indicator Descriptions of Setting Expectations

- Students are informed regarding the objectives, standards, and concepts being taught.
- Students have a clear understanding of what they are going to learn, how they will learn it, and why.

Complete Steps 5, 6, and 7 onsite, and prepare to share at Courageous Leadership Academy (CLA) I Session 3 debriefing.

Step 5: Prepare for the Instructional Learning Walk

1. Review the list of the indicators of quality instruction and your group's description of each.
2. Identify examples of the indicators of quality instruction and calibrate your group. This is done by practicing to make sure you are in alignment with each other regarding what you are looking for.
3. Record your group's indicators of quality instruction on the observation sheet on page 62.

Step 6: Do the Instructional Learning Walk

1. Go on an *instructional learning walk* as a group for 30 minutes.
2. Separate and walk through as many classrooms as you have time for with your observation sheet.
3. Look for indicators of quality instruction in each classroom you visit. (This activity does not expect you to identify either the teacher or students.)
4. Place a check mark next to each indicator that you observe.

Step 7: Debrief the Instructional Learning Walk

Tally the number of times you observed each indicator of quality instruction, first individually and then as a group. Consider the following questions as a form of data:

1. Which indicators were observed most frequently?
2. Which indicators were observed least frequently?
3. Which of the indicators were observed occasionally?

For each of the above questions (data points 1, 2, and 3), also consider

- What conclusions could you draw regarding the quality of instruction in your school?
- What questions are you asking about what you observed?
- What areas of quality would you especially like to celebrate?
- What suggestions do you have for "next steps" in communicating your observations?

Observation Sheet

Check if the behavior is observed in the classroom (CR)

Indicators: Teacher Behavior	CR 1	CR 2	CR 3	CR 4	CR 5	CR 6
Totals						
Indicators: Students Behavior	CR 1	CR 2	CR 3	CR 4	CR 5	CR 6
Totals						

Resource 16. Checklist for Using Diagnostic (Preteaching) Assessments

If you have not been doing diagnostic assessments, use the following checklist to help you get started.

❏ I have made an effort to learn about students' interests and learning styles, ideally at the beginning of the year or semester.

❏ I have used the following methods (e.g., survey, observation, conversation):

Method	Date

❏ I have recorded my results and observations (where?).

❏ I have tried to determine my students' range of knowledge about the topic I'm about to teach.

Method	Date

❏ I have tried to determine my students' misconceptions about the topic I'm about to teach.

Method	Date

❏ In response to my findings, I have adopted the following teaching plans and adaptations:

❏ My students have been informed about our learning goals for this topic or unit.

❏ My students have been told about the assessments and criteria I will use to conclude the unit.

❏ My students have seen examples or models of the performances I will expect of them.

❏ The methods I have used are all nongraded and do not adversely affect students' self-esteem.

The use of diagnostic assessments caused the following changes in my instructional planning:

I would evaluate my experience using diagnostic assessments as follows:

Resource 17. Checklist for Using Formative Assessments

If you have not been using formative assessments, use the following checklist to help you get started.

☐ I am providing feedback to the students frequently throughout the teaching unit. I plan to start teaching the unit on _____ and conclude it on _____. During that period, I will provide feedback by the following methods:

Date	Graded? (Y/N)	Strategies

☐ I have made sure the feedback I provide is very specific.

☐ I have made sure that the students have clearly understood the feedback I give them. The information I have gained has led me to modify my lesson plan in the following way:

☐ My students have been given opportunities to show that they can correct and adjust the quality of their work.

☐ My students have begun to learn to self-assess their own work. Evidence and comments:

My evaluation of my experience with using formative assessments:

Source: Reprinted with permission from *Failure Is Not an Option 3: Effective Assessment for Effective Learning* [Video series]. Bloomington, IN: HOPE Foundation, 2009.

Resource 18. Checklist for Using Summative Assessments

My students will perform summative assessments on _____ *(name of teaching unit)* on _____ *(dates).*

❑ My students have known since the beginning of the unit what kinds of summative performance I expect. The assessments will be aligned with the following learning goals:

❑ The assessments will be authentic. The knowledge and skills that students display are transferrable in the following ways:

❑ I have offered these options *(two or more)* to the students to display their learning, accommodate various learning styles, and target different learning goals:

Task	Learning Style	Targeted Learning Goal
1.		
2.		
3.		

❑ My students are aware of the criteria on which their work or performance will be assessed. I will use the following criteria to assess students' work:

Task	Rubric (Criteria)	Value (% of Grade)
1.		
2.		
3.		

I would evaluate each of the assessment tasks as follows:

- Task 1:
- Task 2:
- Task 3:

Other comments:

Source: Reprinted with permission from *Failure Is Not an Option 3: Effective Assessment for Effective Learning* [Video series]. Bloomington, IN: HOPE Foundation (2009).

Workshop Evaluation Form

Content

- How well did the seminar meet the goals and objectives?

- What professional support will you need to implement what you have learned from this seminar?

- How well did the topics explored in this seminar meet a specific need in your school or district?

- How relevant was this topic to your professional life?

Process

- How well did the instructional techniques and activities facilitate your understanding of the topic?

- How can you incorporate the activities learned today into your daily professional life?

- Were a variety of learning experiences included in the seminar?

- Was any particular activity memorable? What made it stand out?

Context

- Were the facilities conducive to learning?

- Were the accommodations adequate for the activities involved?

Overall

- Overall, how successful would you consider this seminar? Please include a brief comment or explanation.

- What was the most valuable thing you gained from this seminar experience?

Additional Comments

Source: Adapted from *Evaluating Professional Development* by Thomas R. Guskey, Corwin, 2000.

Notes

CORWIN

A SAGE Company

The Corwin logo—a raven striding across an open book—represents the union of courage and learning. Corwin is committed to improving education for all learners by publishing books and other professional development resources for those serving the field of PreK–12 education. By providing practical, hands-on materials, Corwin continues to carry out the promise of its motto: **"Helping Educators Do Their Work Better."**

The HOPE Foundation logo stands for Harnessing Optimism and Potential Through Education. The HOPE Foundation helps to develop and support educational leaders over time at district- and state-wide levels to create school cultures that sustain all students' achievement, especially low-performing students.